D1446203

Take a Closer Look at

Plastic

by JoAnn Early Macken

Content Consultant
Patty Moore
President/CEO
Moore Recycling Associates, Sonoma, CA

RED
CHAIR
•PRESS•™

Please visit our website at **www.redchairpress.com** for more high-quality products for young readers.

About the Author: JoAnn Early Macken has written more than 130 books for young readers. JoAnn earned her M.F.A. in Writing for Children and Young Adults at Vermont College of Fine Arts. She has taught writing at four Wisconsin colleges, and she speaks about poetry and writing to children and adults at schools, libraries, and conferences.

Publisher's Cataloging-In-Publication Data

Macken, JoAnn Early, 1953-
    Take a closer look at. Plastic / by JoAnn Early Macken ; content consultant, Patty Moore, President, Moore Recycling Associates, Sonoma, CA. -- [First edition].

    pages : illustrations, maps, charts ; cm

    Summary: Plastic is everywhere, but some experts say today's plastic will be in our landfills for thousands of years to come. Explore the good and the bad of plastic in our lives and learn how scientists are looking for new ways to produce biodegradable, Earth-friendly plastic substitutes. STEM career opportunities are featured. Includes a glossary and references for additional reading.
    "Core content library"--Cover.
    Interest age level: 006-010.
    Edition statement supplied by publisher.
    Issued also as an ebook. (ISBN: 978-1-63440-058-9)
    Includes bibliographical references and index.
    ISBN: 978-1-63440-050-3 (library hardcover)

    1. Plastics--Social aspects--Juvenile literature. 2. Plastic scrap--Environmental aspects--Juvenile literature. 3. Biodegradable plastics--Juvenile literature. 4. Plastics. 5. Plastic scrap--Environmental aspects. 6. Biodegradable plastics. I. Moore, Patty. II. Title. III. Title: Take a closer look at plastic IV. Title: Plastic

TP1125 .M33 2016
668.4   2015937987

Illustration credits: Joe LeMonnier: 14, 19

Photo credits: Dreamstime: cover, 7(bottom), 16, 17, 29 (bottom insert); iStock photo: Cover, 3; Shutterstock: 1, 4, 5, 6, 7, 8, 9, 10, 12, 13, 15, 17(insert), 18, 20, 21, 22, 23, 24, 25, 26, 27, 28, 29, 30, 31, 32, 33, 34, 35, 36, 37, 38, 39, 40

This series first published by:
Red Chair Press LLC   PO Box 333   South Egremont, MA 01258-0333

Printed in the United States of America
Distributed in the U.S. by Lerner Publisher Services. www.lernerbooks.com

112015 1P LPSS16

Contents

1

How Did We Get to This Point?

Chances are something nearby is made of plastic. It's everywhere, and for good reasons. Plastic is convenient. It's versatile. And it's inexpensive. Many things that used to be made of glass, metal, or leather now come in plastic.

Walk down the aisles in a grocery store. You'll see shelves full of plastic jars, bags, and bottles. Peanut butter and jelly. Catsup and mustard. Yogurt and cheese. Bread, grapes, and salad greens. You can see them through clear plastic. Milk in a plastic jug is light and easy to pour. And less food is wasted because it stays fresh longer. Your shopping cart might be plastic, too!

At home, toddlers drink from sturdy plastic cups. Dolls, blocks, and tub duckies are plastic. Blenders and coffee makers have plastic parts. Plastic keeps picnic food cool in coolers. Car seats, bike helmets, and air bags all help keep us safe. Magazines in the mail? Plastic bags protect their covers.

At school, you'll find plastic pens. Cafeteria tables and chairs are plastic. It's durable enough to use for slides and swings on playgrounds. Parts of computers, keyboards, and mice? You bet—plastic!

In hospitals, plastic saves time and money. Health care workers are safer, too. They can use a syringe once and throw it away. Plastic bags are flexible. They hold blood and other fluids that keep people alive. Plastic tubes carry those fluids to patients. All these products are free from germs.

How many plastic products do you see in a day?

Restaurants serve food on plastic dishes. People eat with plastic utensils. Takeout containers and coffee cup lids? Plastic, of course. It's disposable.

Car parts made from plastic are lighter than metal. For drivers, that saves gas. Lighter weight saves shipping costs, too. Plastic insulates homes. Shrink wrap holds pallets of building supplies. Plastic plumbing and sewer pipes don't rust. Siding and window frames can be plastic, too.

History

Plastic has not been around for long. Celluloid was one early type. It dates back nearly a century and a half. It was used to make film for photographs. Bakelite was invented about forty years later. Telephones and handles on cooking items were made of this durable plastic. Nylon, a type of plastic first made in the 1930s, is used in clothing and tents. Everyday use of plastic grew quickly after World War II.

Making Plastic

How is plastic made today? Most types begin with crude oil or natural gas. Refining breaks it into a number of products. Heat and chemicals turn some of them into plastic types called resins. The resins are shaped into pellets. Colors can be added. Chemicals might make one resin softer. They might help another resist fire. Each resin has a different use.

Before resins can be made into products, they must be heated. Then they can be handled in many ways. Here are some of them.

Plastic pellets ready for reuse

Product	Process
yogurt tubs	Pellets are melted, then forced into a cool mold.
bottles	Pellets are melted, then a glob is lowered into a cool mold. Air is blown into the glob. It pushes the plastic against the walls of the mold.
large, hollow objects like garbage cans	Plastic powder is spread into a rotating mold. The plastic melts against the walls of the mold.
tubes	Pellets are forced through a heated cylinder. A screw revolves in the center. (This process is called extruding.)
flat sheets	Warm extruded plastic is pressed between rollers.
foam cups	Gas is dissolved in the plastic. Heating it inside a mold releases the gas.
bags and plastic film	Melted plastic is extruded or pushed through a tube to form a thin bubble that is then collapsed into flat film.

Recycling Plastic

Recycling plastic mostly means making it into something new. For example, milk jugs are mostly made into new colored containers for laundry detergent. Soda and water bottles are regularly made into new water and soda bottles.

Here are some steps in the recycling process.

1. Plastic is collected at the curb or drop-off center.

2. The plastics are sorted by resin type *(see p. 14)*

3. Sorted plastic is baled and shipped to a reclaimer that:

4. removes labels and bottle caps and further sorts, washes, and grinds plastic into flakes.

The flakes are sorted to remove any contamination. Then, filtered and melted into pellets ready to be used to make new products.

Examples of products made from recycled plastics

Recycling plastic requires many steps to turn it back into new products. Recycling uses less energy than creating new plastic. It also emits lower amounts of **greenhouse gases**. It is easier on Earth. But it does not solve all of plastic's problems.

The Process of Recycled Plastic

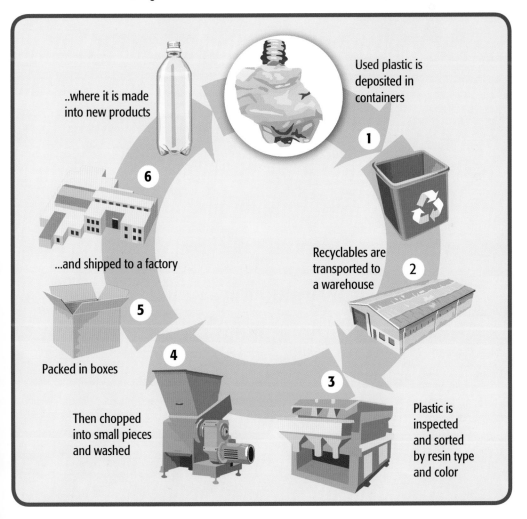

..where it is made into new products

Used plastic is deposited in containers

1

6

Recyclables are transported to a warehouse

2

...and shipped to a factory

5

Packed in boxes

4

3

Plastic is inspected and sorted by resin type and color

Then chopped into small pieces and washed

2 What's the Problem?

Bales of plastic are ready to be cleaned and sorted.

It lasts and lasts...

Plastic's biggest strength might also be its biggest problem. It lasts and lasts. If it is not recycled or disposed of properly it can break into smaller pieces, but it does not go away.

Today most plastic is made from fossil fuels because it is less costly. Crude oil will run out some day. Extracting it, or bringing it out of the ground, becomes harder as supplies are used up. (See *Take a Closer Look at Oil*)

A lot of plastic is tossed in the garbage. (Look around a school cafeteria at lunchtime!) This trash is collected and hauled to landfills. There it piles up, ton upon ton. But the bigger problem might be the lost opportunity to recycle materials lost to garbage.

Some countries in Europe ban postconsumer plastics in landfills and recover more than 90% of the material for recycling or energy production. Until recycling plastics is required across the country, the United States is a long way from reaching this standard.

Plastic Resin ID Codes and Examples

Manufacturers mark some plastic items with codes. These numbers refer to the resins. They help workers separate items after recycling.

Symbol	Number	Abbreviation	Resin Name	Examples
(1) PETE	1	PET, PETE	Polyethylene Terephthalate	water bottles, salad containers
(2)	2	HDPE	High Density Polyethylene	milk bottles, bags, detergent bottles
(3) V	3	PVC, V	Polyvinyl Chloride	pipes
(4) LDPE	4	LDPE, LLDPE	Low Density Polyethylene, Linear Low Density Polyethylene	squeeze bottles, bread bags, laundry baskets
(5) PP	5	PP	Polypropylene	bottles, dairy tubs, cups
(6) PS	6	PS	Polystyrene	insulated food trays
(7) OTHER	7	Other	Other Resin Types	sports gear

Types 1-6 indicate items found in most homes. Type 7 is used for mixtures and anything else.

Many cities collect all plastic items. But many collect only a few types. Not everything collected can be recycled. Some resins have ready markets. Others have no place to go. No one wants them.

Most plastic items can be recycled. But many are not. Many cities and towns have banned the use of *expanded polystyrene* or EPS. Polystyrene is one of the most common forms of plastic, often called by the brand name Styrofoam. It is a packing material used in shipping goods. It is often used in take-out coffee cups, egg cartons and meat trays from the supermarket. Because it is light in weight, it is hard to collect from curbside containers. Polystyrene often blows away, becoming litter. Because it's bulky, it is difficult and expensive to transport. Many town recycling programs do not accept it (a few, like Los Angeles and Toronto, do).

When EPS and single-use plastic bags are banned by cities and towns, it can be good for reducing litter. But it often reduces the number of retail collection sites for these items. Where will residents drop off plastic bags and packaging from dry-cleaning, bread, or toilet paper?

Type of Plastic Waste	% Recycled in the U.S.
bottles marked 1	31%
containers marked 2	28%
plastic bags	12%
total U.S. plastic waste	9%

Source: Environmental Protection Agency, 2012 data

15

Chemicals in Plastic

Phthalates make plastics softer. **BPA** makes plastics harder. Studies show that they may have health risks. Phthalates are used less often today. Studies are being conducted on the effects of BPA. But for most of us, the risks may be low. Some plastics contain lead, which is poisonous. All these **additives** have been in the news. Some producers changed their formulas. But the new ingredients could be worse. Manufacturers are not required to prove that chemicals in their products are safe.

Workers who make plastic products handle many chemicals. In years past, workers complained about dust and fumes in their workplaces. Studies showed there was an increased risk of cancer and other health problems among workers in plastic plants.

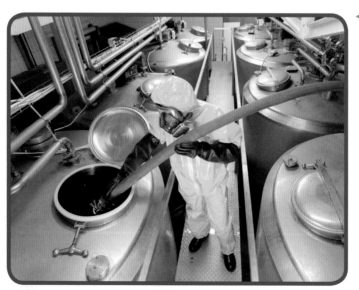

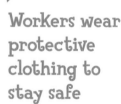

Workers wear protective clothing to stay safe in plastics plants.

Some researchers say chemicals can leak out of plastic products. In a landfill, the chemicals could end up in waterways. The problem is worse when some plastic is heated. (To be safe, it is never a good idea to cook or reheat food in plastic!)

On the Loose

Plastic is lightweight. If we let it loose, wind blows it around. Bags catch in trees. Litter runs to rivers and streams when it rains. Rivers flow into oceans. Plastic washes up on beaches, creating an ugly mess. In the oceans, currents carry plastic. Plastic collects and swirls in these convergence zones.

A volunteer cleans up trash that washed ashore on a beach in Vietnam.

To a turtle, a plastic bag looks like a jellyfish. Turtles eat plastic bags and die. Their insides block up. To a bird, plastic bits look like fish eggs. Birds eat them and feed them to their young. Their guts fill up, and they starve to death.

Floating plastic can also absorb toxins. **DDT** and **PCBs,** both banned, still seep into water. Plastic soaks them up. When an animal eats toxins, they build up in its body. Large animals eat smaller ones and all their toxins. People eat large animals and all the toxins they've eaten.

Five Ocean Whirlpools (Gyres) of Garbage

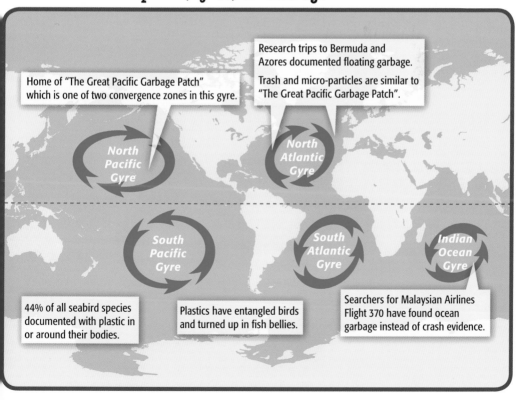

Research trips to Bermuda and Azores documented floating garbage.

Trash and micro-particles are similar to "The Great Pacific Garbage Patch".

Home of "The Great Pacific Garbage Patch" which is one of two convergence zones in this gyre.

North Pacific Gyre

North Atlantic Gyre

South Pacific Gyre

South Atlantic Gyre

Indian Ocean Gyre

44% of all seabird species documented with plastic in or around their bodies.

Plastics have entangled birds and turned up in fish bellies.

Searchers for Malaysian Airlines Flight 370 have found ocean garbage instead of crash evidence.

3 What Can We Do to Help?

Reuse, Recycle

Remember the saying, "Reduce, Reuse, Recycle."

- If you are concerned about the environment, try to use less stuff. Don't buy products with excess packaging. Some single-serve snack bags come inside an outer bag. To save packaging, buy a larger size. Pack snacks in your own containers. Use them again. Don't use cosmetics and soaps with tiny plastic beads. The beads end up in the ocean.

- Reuse what you can or give it away. People often donate items to Goodwill® or local thrift stores. Those things stay out of landfills. People who take them save money.

- Recycle more plastic. Find out which types are collected at your home and school. Help stop the growth of plastic islands in oceans! Give sea creatures a better chance to survive! Place your plastics in the bin. Keep plastic bags out of trees! Bring them back to the grocery store to recycle. And remember: Never litter!

Small steps add up if enough people take them. Here are some more ways you can help.

Most things we use don't need to last forever. They don't need to be plastic. Cardboard makes a sturdy cover for a school notebook. Powder laundry soap comes in cardboard boxes. A stainless steel water bottle can be washed and reused. Tap water might be better for you than bottled water.

Will young children handle bottles of juice? If not, glass could be a better choice. (Most juice boxes are lined with plastic.) If you buy soft drinks, look for cans. They can be recycled into more cans. Use bar soap instead of bottled. Look for paper egg cartons, not foam.

Bamboo is a **renewable** resource. It's made into dishes, clothing, and even floors. Hemp is another fast-growing plant. It's also used in clothing. Try other natural fabrics such as wool and cotton. Look for wooden toys. Cloth shower curtains. Furniture made of metal or wood.

Paper or plastic? Some communities have banned single-use plastic bags. Both paper and plastic shopping bags pile up in landfills. They both require energy to produce.

2 Use more Earth-friendly plastics.

Scientists are working to develop bioplastics, made from plants. You might find water or soft drinks in bottles made partly from bioplastics.

Some bioplastics can be **composted** under special conditions. In high temperatures, they break down in about 45 days.

Some new plastics have additives to make them **biodegradable.** This means they can be broken down by **microorganisms.** But they are not made from plants like bioplastics.

Bioplastics can usually be recycled with other plastics.

Both can pollute air and water when they are manufactured. Carry cloth shopping bags. Reuse them proudly. You are helping the Earth.

Bio-based plastic can be made from wood or any of these plants:

- corn
- potatoes
- rice
- sugar beets
- sugar cane
- sweet potatoes
- tapioca
- wheat

NATURAL
100%
BIODEGRADABLE
NATURAL

Artists in The Gambia crochet purses out of used plastic bags. Volunteers in Chicago use plastic bags to make sleeping mats. They give them to homeless people. In Chile, plastic fishing nets are made into skateboards.

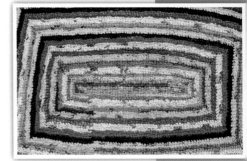

Make Good Choices

- Buy used items when you can.

- Share things you use only sometimes.

- Use cloth napkins and towels instead of paper.

- Carry a reusable lunch box and cloth bags.

26

Some of these products also contain recycled plastic.

- TVs
- cameras
- computers
- measuring cups
- toys
- lunch bags
- flower pots

- backpacks
- sports jerseys
- shoes
- toothbrushes
- soap bottles
- shampoo bottles
- plastic hangers

Look for clothes made from natural fabrics like cotton.

When plastic is not properly disposed of it can become litter and end up scattered on beaches and streets. Take part in beach cleanups. Where you see plastic (or any) litter, help pick it up.

Does your school have a recycling program? If not, why not start one? The plastic you save to recycle might become a fleece jacket or lawn chair.

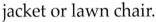

28

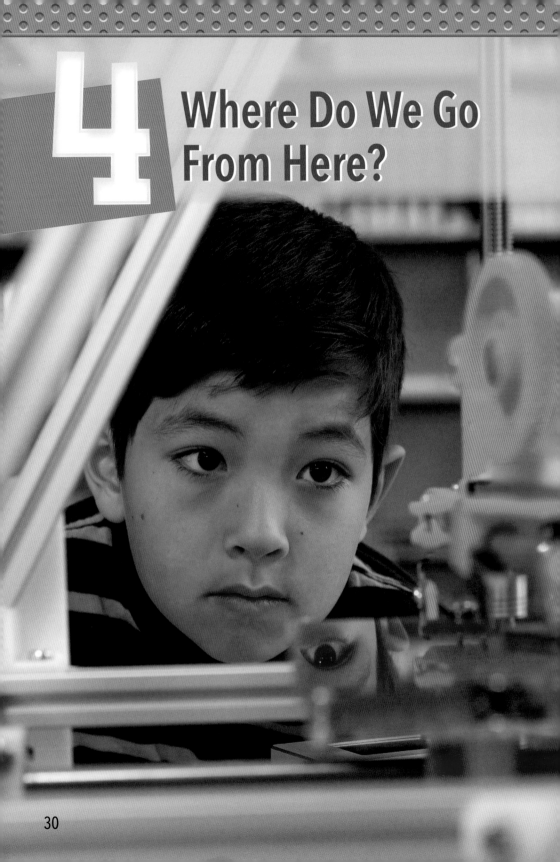

4 Where Do We Go From Here?

New uses for plastic keep popping up. It could help bring down the cost of solar panels. New plastic light bulbs don't shatter. Huge plastic balloons could provide Internet service to remote locations.

3-D printers use plastic. The process wastes little. It adds layer on layer rather than cutting away scrap. It might save shipping costs. People can make their own products closer to where they are needed. It might also save time.

Back to Oil

New businesses are gearing up to turn plastic back into oil. They melt the plastic without oxygen. Chemicals burn up. They leave a small amount of residue called char. (Is it safe? Business owners say yes.) This process could keep millions of tons of plastic out of landfills. It might even use plastics that can't be recycled. Plastic could produce fuel to drive millions of cars. It could generate electricity to heat millions of homes.

31

New Ways to Make Plastic

AirCarbon plastics are made with carbon pulled out of the air. The process starts with methane gas from landfills and dairy farms. It removes more carbon than it emits. It is already being used to make cell phone cases.

New Ways to Recycle

A waxworm is a moth larva that eats plastic. Scientists have found that bacteria in its gut can break down plastic. They hope that this research will lead to new ways to get rid of plastic waste.

Engineers are working on a new way to sort, clean, and melt plastics with chemicals. The process could take minutes rather than hours. It might also produce a better quality of plastic.

A researcher invented a machine called a RecycleBot. Now he shreds his own used milk jugs. With the plastic, he creates the filament used in 3D printers.

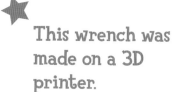
This wrench was made on a 3D printer.

Recovery

Tons of plastic float in our oceans. People keep looking for ways to remove it. One young diver invented a method that could help. He plans to build a series of barriers that float. They will  collect plastic as it circles through the ocean **gyres**. In ten years, The Ocean Cleanup could remove half the plastic in the largest gyre. After that, it could add floating barriers in rivers.

What Would We Do Without Plastic?

Without plastic, we may have more oil for fuel. But our vehicles would be heavier and use more fuel. We'd have less trash flying around. But we might waste more food if it couldn't stay as fresh. More people might become ill from infectious diseases if using unclean syringes.

Some plastic products are the best options we have. Others can be replaced with safer materials. Someday soon, maybe they will be. That could be good news for the planet— and for us. But it is not enough.

Use Plastic Wisely

Plastic is certainly useful. Convenient. And cheap—in the short term. In the long term, it can be costly. We cannot afford—our planet cannot bear—some of the ways we use it now. We cannot keep using so much plastic and throwing it away!

We all must do what we can. Decide where plastic is really needed. Use it wisely. Dispose of it carefully. Remember the three Rs. And add a few more. Rethink. Refuse. Refill. Recover.

Help spread the word. Ask your friends and family to reduce, reuse, and recycle plastic. Ask store owners to skip extra packaging. Bring your plastic bags and containers back to the store. Most will accept them for recycling.

We have a long way to go. But there is hope! You might see some of these problems solved in your lifetime. You can start helping now. What will you do?

STEM Career Connections

All over the world, workers are needed in four key areas:

- Science
- Technology
- Engineering
- Math

Scientists work in research labs. They also go out in the world to observe. They collect data to study. Technology puts science to practical use. Many STEM jobs are related to computers. Engineers solve problems. They invent and design new products. Math is a key skill in many kinds of jobs.

The plastic industry keeps growing. It will need trained workers for some time to come. They'll use math to figure out costs. They'll study science data.

Think up new theories. Explore safer materials. Document methods. They might focus on these and other issues:

- making plastic from plants without harming the food supply
- cutting pollution from production and recycling
- recovering used plastic from homes, oceans and landfills

STEM skills help people working with plastic and its uses in these fields.

- aerospace
- automotive
- biotechnology
- construction
- energy
- healthcare
- information technology
- manufacturing
- transportation

How will plastic fit into your future?

Resources

Books

One Plastic Bag: Isatou Ceesay and the Recycling Women of the Gambia by Miranda Paul. Millbrook Press (2015)

Plastic (What Happens When We Recycle) by Jillian Powell. Franklin Watts Ltd. (2014)

Plastic, Ahoy!: Investigating the Great Pacific Garbage Patch by Patricia Newman. Millbrook Press (2014)

Tracking Trash: Flotsam, Jetsam, and the Science of Ocean Motion (Scientists in the Field Series) by Loree Griffin Burns. HMH Books for Young Readers (2010)

Trash Talk: Moving Toward a Zero-Waste World by Michelle Mulder. Orca Book Publishers (2015)

Web Sites and Videos

How is plastic made from petroleum? (Highlights Kids)
http://www.highlightskids.com/science-questions/how-plastic-made-petroleum

Plastic Facts (Kids Go Green):
http://your.caerphilly.gov.uk/kidsgogreen/fact-zone/plastic-facts

The Ocean Cleanup: http://www.theoceancleanup.com/

Glossary

additive: a substance added to another substance in a small amount to produce an effect

biodegradable: able to be broken down by natural processes

BPA: Bisphenol A, a chemical added to polycarbonate, which is used to make hard plastic water bottles and other containers. BPA is also used in the linings of metal food cans. It has been banned from use in some products made for children.

compost: to collect plant material so it can break down and be used to improve soil

DDT: an insecticide that is now banned in the United States

greenhouse gas: a gas that traps heat in the atmosphere. Most greenhouse gases come from burning coal, natural gas, and oil. Greenhouse gases contribute to climate change.

gyre: a circular whirl of ocean current**microorganisms:** living things that are too small to be seen without a microscope

PCBs: chemicals formerly used in industry that are now banned in the United States

phthalates: chemicals used to make plastics softer and more flexible. They are also called plasticizers. Phthalates have been shown to interfere with hormone functions. Some types are banned from use in products made for children.

renewable: able to be replaced by nature

Index